Baby you can drive my car...

Michèle Praeger

BLUE LIGHT PRESS ◆ 1ST WORLD PUBLISHING

1st WORLD
PUBLISHING

SAN FRANCISCO ◆ FAIRFIELD ◆ DELHI

Baby you can drive my car...

Copyright ©2015 by Michèle Praeger

1ST WORLD LIBRARY
PO Box 2211
Fairfield, Iowa 52556
www.1stworldpublishing.com

BLUE LIGHT PRESS
www.bluelightpress.com
Email: bluelightpress@aol.com

BOOK & COVER DESIGN
Melanie Gendron

COVER ART
"Le Vélo de Tati" by Robert Doisneau.
(c) Robert Doisneau/Rapho.
Used by permission of Isabelle Satys

AUTHOR PHOTO
Catrina Bevilacqua

FIRST EDITION

Library of Congress Control Number: 2015916256

ISBN 9781421837420

Baby you can drive my car...

Contents

"Baby, you can drive my car…"

I sing this to myself. So cool…"Baby," that's how guys call girls in America. Here, only my father can drive *his* car. "Baby, you can drive my car…" How extraordinary!

I come to the dinner table in my black turtle neck sweater and pants, under the disapproving gaze of my father. His mustache is bristling. Why can't I dress like a girl?

Why does he care? Doesn't he have anything better to do than torment me?

Bob Dylan sings, "How does it feel to be like a rolling stone?" How original, how daring! My friends at school say that Dylan is singing, "I like the Rolling Stones." I know that's not what Dylan means, but I let it go; I don't want to appear a know-it-all.

My aunt is a nurse at the American Hospital in Paris. They have a PX where she buys American products at a discount. When she visits us in the suburbs, she brings "Baby Ruth" chocolate bars, covered with crunchy peanuts and filled with a caramel paste that sticks to your fingers. They taste like Paradise. Nobody knows what "Baby Ruth" means, including my aunt. I laugh because my mother's name is Ruth.

My mother says that when she was a child, a family of Americans moved into the house next door. When they finished with a can of food, they just threw it out the back window. There was a big pile in their backyard. She says they wanted to adopt her and take her back to America! That makes us all laugh.

My aunt claims that at Christmas, Americans cook the turkey with marshmallows. When the bird comes out of the oven, they pour honey over it and sprinkle it with cornflakes! Really? How amazing, these Americans!

My brother says that he heard on the radio that when the ashtray in their car is full, Americans buy a new car. We marvel.

My father states that when an American woman breaks a nail, she has a tantrum! He says that American women can divorce their husbands for "mental cruelty." Even my mother chuckles at the joke.

When I visit my aunt at the American Hospital, I feel I am in a friendly foreign country. People smile and make a fuss about me, even though I am wearing my eternal black turtle neck and black pants. One male nurse even says to my aunt that I am "cute." "Cute" I have never heard this adjective; I have never been labeled "cute." Now he's calling me "baby!" When I leave, they load me up with chewing gum and Baby Ruth, and wave cheery good-byes.

These Americans are much nicer than the French. One day I'll move to America!

Whiteness and its Shadows

You find yourself sitting inside a white cube, on a white ottoman shaped like a cube. You have no idea how you got there.

You are wearing white, surrounded by white walls. The northern wall hosts a white board; a white ceiling hovers over you. The wooden floor has been covered with glossy white deck paint.

The cube now appears to you as spherical, inviting. The white angular corners have softened into curves. You settle comfortably on the ottoman, which has rounded, but you keep a straight back.

From the white rolled-up screen above the white blackboard, a white string hangs and reflects on the board's white shiny surface. You stare at the string and its darker reflection.

You remember a tale about a cave in which prisoners are chained, facing the wall across from the opening. These creatures perceive their own shadows on the rocky wall and those of illuminated objects behind them. They mistake these forms for reality and act accordingly, shortsightedly. As humans do.

You turn around to face the southern wall and see your own shadow. And you wonder which person, the one in white or her darker shadow, is the true "you."

Do Babies Think?

In commemoration of Descartes' 418th Birthday

The Big Bang does not signal the beginning of time and space! Before the Big Bang, there was cosmic inflation which is responsible for the Big Bang. The Big Bang is not a *cause* but a *consequence*. But what was there *before* cosmic inflation? They still don't know.

Analogically, my first memory corresponds to the cosmic Big Bang. Before my first memory, what am I?

What was I *before* the first event I remember? Is my first event-memory the consequence of inflation of what preceded the creation of my ego? Is the birth of my ego a result of a big bang, preceded by an inflation? And an inflation of what? What was there *before* the birth of my ego, and do I already have an ego? Or am I still pure id?

I have to keep all this to myself because I can't talk yet. I scream piercing cries and I whimper. I am in a panic. My ears are ringing. I'm agitated. The crib rocks from side to side.

Mommy is looking over me with her Mona Lisa smile. She firmly stops the rocking motion, uncovers her breast, picks me up and gently brings me to her. I am loved; therefore, I am. *Amata sum, ergo sum.*

The Bill She Forgot to Pay

Antigone is on edge tonight. She is pacing the sidewalks, in one of the red-light district of Paris. Rue Saint-Denis was named after the first bishop of Paris, but its route dates from the Romans. It is crowned by the Porte Saint Denis designed by Louis XIV to honor his victories; its frontispiece bears the gilded bronze inscription: LUDOVICO MAGNO.

Antigone is practicing the oldest profession in the world, but only one night out of two. Tomorrow for instance, Oscar, her best friend and confidante, is taking her to *La Coupole*. She is dying for oysters — the special kind which can only be consumed in the months with r's. Then, they'll go dancing at the Palace.

So there she is — smoking a Benson & Hedges and letting her gaze float over what is available. A Japanese tourist? The kind eager to film their encounter — and oblivious to her. A Russian widower, an uncouth and brutal *muzhik*? A provincial judge attending a conference in the capital? She exhales a delicate cloud of blue smoke. She wants a different experience.

She sees him across the street — a tall, rangy, rugged individual under a white cowboy hat and boots to match! He has the air of Gary Cooper in *High Noon*; a decent fellow, no doubt, with feelings. He has style. Their eyes lock.

On her green stiletto heels, she deftly crosses the damp street which now reflects red, green and white lights. Boldly, in her Parisian way, she stands in front of him, her pink lips close to his chest: "Baby? Tonight?"

The cowboy's big blue eyes have taken an air of distress. It is obvious he does not understand her English. She points to herself: "Me, Antigone" and then to him: "You?" The cowboy's tense jaw open ups in a huge, toothy grin: "Me? Bill."

They climb the narrow staircase, he following the green sinuosity of her body. She unlocks the door with a little golden key.

And here is Antigone, on her side, naked with her long alabaster back to him, her head turned towards him, faintly smiling, her Venetian hair now cascading freely over her shoulders. She's a nymph; he's a shepherd. Everything vibrates and envelopes them.

In the morning, she is asleep, a Mona Lisa smile on her lips. He gets up without delay in his American way. Moving his shoulders in a vigorous roll of trapezoidal muscles, he puts on his plaid shirt, deftly slips into his jeans — attracting attention to his magnificent quadriceps and abductors. Now his black leather boots, with Native American cutouts, in yellow leather, find their way to his bare feet. He picks up his hat from the floor and dusts it with a flip of his hand.

He sits by the side of Antigone lying in supine abandon on the disheveled bed. He kisses her in a fold of her neck, on the tip of her left breast. she wakes up and sees that he is looking at her intently. He says, "Baby, you owe me." She looks back at him, in dismay. He offers this, "You wouldn't want Oscar, my lover, to laugh at me when I told him the story. He would say 'Ah, ah the Bill she forgot to pay!'"

Metempsychosis

My skin is dry and leathery. I have warts in hidden places. I like dark and swampy places. My body soaks in the lukewarm muddy waters. Only my eyes and my wrinkled forehead emerge. I have a wrinkly forehead because I think a lot, being a solitary creature.

At night, I look at the stars, which are so twinkly and removed that they are intimidating. I once heard two lovers sitting on a bench not far from where I was making bubbles in the water, illuminated by the moon. He was saying, as she admiringly gazed at him, that the stars that shine the brightest are already dead and that their reflection is just reaching us. I suppose that by "us" he meant "us, humans" without thinking (how human!) that more humble creatures could also be awed by the wonders of the firmament.

In my next reincarnation, I would like to be an astronomer or a philosopher or both, as there used to be in the XVII Century. An astronomer because I would have access to telescopes to observe the celestial beings; a philosopher because I would reflect upon the infinity of space and the limitations of humans.

But who is "I"? you may ask. An intermediary being, between a toad and a philosopher? A being, just a being, with bulging eyes and glasses sitting at the terrace of a café, reflecting on the mysteries of life while savoring my afternoon espresso.

The Long Hello

Big bustle at the El Al counter at Kennedy. A group from Brown University is leaving for a trip to Israel. Here's Sophie, wearing torn jeans, a white T-shirt, a Star of David and a Palestinian scarf. She is a Jewish French (or French Jewish) exchange student. She doesn't care what form God may take.

Drew, the other character of the story, is dressed as a Hasidic Jew.

Their eyes meet, and flash. They're in conflicted love.

"Hello, I'm Sophie. You're also from Brown?"

She admires his ivory skin and his dark unruly curls. What a contrast! And his dark habit, black hat, white shirt with all those strings, what do they call them? What do they do with them?

He shrugs. "So why you're going to Israel?" he asks defiantly. "To bring back salts from the Dead Sea?"

Sophie has ambivalent feelings towards the sarcasm, but it does have an edge. She answers, "I'm spending most of my time in Jaffa doing research on expropriated Palestinians."

"Figures!" he snorts ironically "I'm going to Jerusalem to teach a seminar at Hebrew University."

"Figures!" she retorts, not missing a beat, "On Being Holier than Thou?"

He smiles enchantingly. Now he looks very young. Now he looks like he could be fun.

"But for how long?" she wonders. Why does she worry? She doesn't want to marry anyway. Why not have a fling with a Hasid? Will he call her a whore because she doesn't shave her head or take purifying bathes? Will he burn her Palestinian scarf, the crown of her possessions? Will he force her to convert and wash his feet?

"But, are you really from Brown?" she's dying to ask.

He's staring at her with inquisitive black eyes.

Meanwhile, the plane to the Promised Land takes off.

Do Clothes Make the Person?

Naked, given differences in size and gender, we pretty much all look alike. Clothes are our definition. Whether you are mad about romantic thrills, à la Jessica McClintock or into sleek Urban Chic, clothes express — and even create — the self. It does not need to be a whole outfit. An accessory suffices: a hat placed sideways in curly short hair, a pair of boots with silver buckles, a star-studded belt, an iridescent silk scarf circling a neck can subtly signal the real self buried under routine and conformity.

Some people dress conventionally during the day, but at night they transform through their clothes. Instead of his somber day suit, Didier — hopping from club to club — wears a pink T-shirt, tight black leather pants, cowboy boots, and displays rings of fake diamonds on every one of his red-gloved fingers. Noah has traded his corduroy brown pants and plaid shirt for a gold lame dress, green high-heeled sandals, and a shimmering feather boa. Nicole has discarded her stewardess' uniform for a Charlie Chaplin tramp look. She is herself at long last: she walks like a duck, rolls her eyes and oscillates her cane, while gratifying company with a shy and sly smile.

Here comes Nancy, the best dressed woman in America. She owns dresses, coats, shirts, hats, shoes, belts designed with her in mind by the most famous couturiers: Yves Saint-Laurent, Jean Paul Gautier, Christian Lacroix, in the most exquisite colors and fabric. She is ready for any contingency. Nancy is never caught looking unkempt. She has an outfit for every day of every season, for every event of every night, such as Tuesday nights at the Opera or the Black and White Ball. She is smiling while people admire her most recent outfit. "How tasteful!" they exclaim, "How discerning! How extraordinary!"

But somebody whispers: Nancy is naked! Indeed her head, her neck, her torso, her legs, her buttocks, her feet, her hands have been freed from the tyranny of the stylists. Like Venus stepping out of her shell, she daintily moves a pink bare foot; her toenails are devoid of varnish. And her hair is loosely dancing around her freshly washed face. She turns towards her best friend and murmurs, "I have never felt so much myself. I am a natural woman after all!"

Elevator Wait

Words are flying helplessly. She is trying to capture them, re-integrate them into their home, her satchel.

He is here, facing her. She did not see him come out of his office. "You forgot those, Ms. Taylor," he says with gravity, a blue stack of onion skin papers marked with her hand-written notes.

She is caught in his talking gaze: we have met at last. Oh where have you been? Where are you off to? Don't leave, yet you can't stay. I have found you only to lose you.

He must have handed her the papers. She must have taken them and placed them in her satchel.

The elevator stops at the 105th floor with a hushed and sudden thump. Her heart rushes to her mouth and goes down as quickly to her toes. Shall I enter and turn my back to him? In a nanosecond. Faces staring blankly at her. She turns around towards where he was standing, an eternity ago. The plane hits the North tower.

The Shifting Sea

We live in a town by the Atlantic. We play in and out of musty bunkers abandoned by the Germans during World War II, massive grey shelters built of stone reinforced by concrete to withstand the Allies' invasion. Bunkers half swallowed up by sand whirling and hurling in spiraled wizard-like shapes, at great speed over the immense beach, desolate and bleak.

We have repeatedly been warned not to pick up — under any circumstances — alluring pens lying on the beach, as they contain little bombs targeted at children. "Such is the barbarity of the Germans," insisted our Mother with her Mona Lisa lips lingering upon us, illuminating us.

When the tide is low, you can't see the ocean, but you can still feel its menacing power. Every year, holiday-makers from Paris are found floating on top of waves, drowned. We follow the receding tide, hip-hopping over the sand, which is becoming hard and wavy underfoot. People come out to hunt shrimp, pants and skirts tucked up, backs bent, pails in hand, meticulously combing the vast field conceded for a few hours by the ocean.

Once, when I was six month old, my mother left me on the beach to jump into the ocean at high tide. Perhaps I went to sleep, lulled by a ray from the sun, an unusually soft maritime breeze. When I woke up, the sand was hard, the sky menacing, the ocean nowhere to be seen. Everything was plunged in dark grey. No Maman in sight. The wind was shaking me, threatening to topple me, nose in the sand quivering with surging mollusk life.

Then she was here, on the unwelcoming wet sand. Was she crying or laughing? Her long slender body shaken by fits. From time to time she turned her grateful face towards me — this tiny oval shaped bundle. The apple of my mother's eye.

Oedipa in Marin

You should have seen me way back when — platform heels made of cork, bright orange straps enhanced with emerald green diamond-shaped studs. Strutting on Broadway and 125th, chest thrown out, defiant gaze. Showing off. We'd swing in those days. That's how we call them now, those days. We'd get into a cab, ask the driver if he's OK with us smoking a joint in the back-seat. Sure, he'd nod, and could he have a hit too.

Times and places have changed. Forget about showing off shoes. Now everybody wears Nikes, even with evening clothes. Really! Now, when you enter a house, it is written over a statue of Buddha, "Please Remove your Shoes, Namaste!" Even before you ring the bell.

Remove the apples of my toes? My Maud Frizons of Paris Python skin? Remove my faux leopards lined with black alligator skin, my satin violet with gold leather appliqué, my black leather and their pearly grey snake overlay? Conversation pieces in themselves. Now they just get dumped helter-skelter next to grubby running shoes or worse, rubber turquoise flip-flops!

Now everybody is reduced to their socks. Socks with holes, socks with fluff stuck to the big toe, socks that don't match.

But how oh how do you compliment people on their socks? Nice socks you got there! Man, you're wearing some cool socks. Great job your mother-in-law did there. Yeah, yeah, she's also into weaving and dog rescuing. Oh no! And you have to keep wearing your toothbrush smile until the muscles in your cheeks ache.

What if you don't wear socks? Then, you have to expose your feet, your craggy feet, your blistering feet, your swollen, faithful, fateful feet to the eyes of strangers.

The Persistence of Memory

He invited his mother to dinner at eight pm, on the first Wednesday of the month. Eight pm, the fateful hour when he watched the current dictator, perched on a Louis XVI chair, deliver his monthly speech on the governmental TV station.

He would stare at the despot, while his mother (his sainted mother!) struggled through the Irish stew which had been simmering in a large pot since mid-morning. Cunégonde, the cook, had already eaten alone, sitting at the kitchen table. She had served herself a large portion of the stringy beef — or was it mutton? — floating in a grey-yellow broth. For desert, she had carefully wiped off the sauce from her plate with a piece of rustic bread, turned the plate upside down and crushed a banana on top. Dreamily, she ate it with an antique silver fork.

His poor suffering mother! She was illegally blind and her mind was going soft, yet he loved her. After all, she had given him life, a miserable life to be sure. Was it better not to have existed at all?

Now, the dictator was looking directly at his mother. His voice went up an octave. He paused; Mom caught her breath. "Happy Mother's Day," he screamed while lifting his long arms to the sky, "to all women who have given sons and daughters to our country," he conceded. "It's a day to rejoice, the Day of the Happy Mother!"

"What is he saying?" shouted Mom to her son.

"Nothing much, Mom. He is thanking you for having given Absurdistan a son."

"Ha Ha," exclaimed Mother, "an ungrateful son who refused to join the army like his heroic father, a son who hasn't given me a grandson, a ne'er do well, an artist, maybe worse!"

She was so upset that she choked on a bone and expired while the dictator gave his final salute to the nation: "God bless Absurdistani mothers. God bless Absurdistan!"

He got up, walked over to his mother's body slumped in the Irish stew. He stroked her back tenderly. He cried bitterly. Now, he was orphan!

Riding with Buddha to Kathmandu's Airport

Mr. Buddha, why are you laughing in one of your avatars? What is the laughing Buddha laughing at? The fact that he just had a good meal of chapattis and vegetable curry? You are often represented with a big belly, Mr. Buddha. Do you find the scene of the world highly comical?

Why does Buddha laugh?

Buddha, who is at the wheel of the taxi, turns his head around. "My dear lady," he answers, "I am laughing because, although I expressly disowned any statue of me being made, people are shopping for buddhas to put in their gardens. As if an idol could bring them peace. Peace is deep within them, if only they could sit in stillness, with a mind devoid of thoughts."

Now we are at the airport. Buddha asks me which airline I am flying. I answer "Buddha Air." He turns around, smiles enigmatically, and wishes me an enlightened journey.

Sins and Absolutions

This Thursday, we are going to confession for the first time. We enter the deserted building. It's damp and dark inside; unlike Sundays, when illuminated as a grand ship, the church displays its stained glass windows of sapphire, crimson and buttery yellows.

A moist atmosphere of grey furtiveness envelopes us now. A nun — white winged wimple, wavy black dress — curtly tells us to sit on the communal blonde wood benches polished by centuries.

A child steps into an elongated box. It has the shape of a London phone booth but is sculpted in dark oak with scenes representing the four seasons in medieval France. We only see the soles of shoes and ankles of our comrade; his head has been engulfed by the dark. A slow psalmody comes from the box — an old man's conciliatory voice, a panicked infantile one. Each word blends into the next, so that nothing makes sense to us. It's endless, but now we clearly hear "Amen!" Then see our comrade, pale and dazed, step out of the box.

My turn. I walk with a heavy heart towards the sinister box. I am not sure what to do except kneel on the dark wooden steps. My face is close to a window with a thick wooden trellis, which cuts up into small lozenges the soft pink face and white hair of the old parish priest. How did he get in the box?

"My child, have you sinned?" He turns his profile, his withered ear towards my face. No words come out of my mouth. "Have you been negligent in saying your prayers at night?"

"No."

"Have you disobeyed your mother?"

"No."

"Have you lied?"

"No."

"Have you ever stolen? "

"No."

"Not even a lump of sugar or a piece of chocolate from your mother?"

"No, no, no."

I hope he won't ask me about the worst of all sins — a mortal sin — "have you ever missed mass?" I have to answer "yes" at least once before the end of the ordeal. Otherwise, I won't appear believable. I had not realized that the litany of sins went crescendo.

But his face bears a benign smile. He marks my forehead with a small sign of the cross. "You are a good little girl, go in peace." How can he say that when I lied the whole time for fear of retribution? I am confused and relieved.

On second thought, he turns his head to face mine and says, "And you'll recite three Paters and four Aves."

Tourist or Terrorist?

I had been hired by the FBI as part of the maritime anti-terror unit based in San Francisco. There had been rumors that Al Qaeda would be targeting famous European monuments such as the Eiffel Tower, Big Ben, the Brandenburg Gate, and even the Pyramids! Would their next target be the Golden Gate Bridge?

My boss, retired admiral Rob Johnson, had posted undercover agents along the bridge to spot planes or bomb-loaded cars eager to destroy our beloved icon. He had assigned me to ride all the ferries back and forth to Sausalito. Some people say that the ferries don't actually go under the bridge, but I maintain they do.

I had been doing this all day long and was feeling tired and nauseous. The food served on the ferry was inedible, and I could not spare enough time to have a decent meal in Sausalito. The tourists were huddling on the deck, shivering and dancing on one foot and the other, underdressed as if they were in Southern California. You would think that with the Internet, they would know better by now. What would we do if we didn't have the tourists to kick around? I sighed in boredom.

It was on my last trip to Sausalito on the lower deck that I spotted a bearded man wearing a blue silk Islamic cap and an embroidered caftan. Uh, I thought… he looks just out of central casting. Unlike most tourists, he had selected the lower level, perhaps simply to protect himself from the fog and wind, or for some more sinister purpose, such as detonating dynamite he had placed around his waist.

I sat facing him, pretending to listen to "Philosophy Talk" on my IPod with Ken Taylor and John Perry, the program that questions everything… Except your intelligence! The man had also taken an IPod out of one of his deep pockets and was nodding his head in appreciation, perhaps of an inflamed speech about the merits of jihad on ferries. Sometimes though, he would shake his head in denegation. I was not sure if shaking his head from left to right meant "no" or "yes," as I had read that in some Russian tribes, they shake their head from left to right for "yes" and backward and forward for "no."

Now, the man was muttering to himself in classical Arabic. Was he looking forward to being welcomed by eighty-six virgins, once he had sent himself and all of us on the ferry — tourists, terrorists, and spies — *ad patres*? And also destroyed the bridge and all cars and bicycles on it. A cold sweat came upon me.

Fog horns sounded resonated. We were sailing under the belly of the Northwestern span; I spotted one of the massive towers. I could hear the rumbling and moaning of the cables which keep the bridge in suspension. The man's black and thick eyes-brows met in the middle of his forehead. His hand went into his pocket. He took out a handkerchief and proceeded to blow his nose. He glanced slyly at me.

Was he going to knife me before he detonated the bomb, just out of spite or perhaps out of kindness? I closed my eyes, wondering if I would see my whole life in reverse, as we are supposed to just before death.

No more creaking or moaning. Silence. We had passed under the bridge. I sighed and I opened my eyes. My fists were clenched, my shoulders stiff with tension. I slowly unwound like a paper flower in water. He was still there, with his IPod, nodding "yes" or "no."

He looked at me directly. In gently accented English he said, "I think we are listening to the same program, as you have been moving your head the same way I have." I asked tentatively: "Philosophy Talk?" A broad and luminescent smile came upon his black-bearded face. "The program that questions everything, everything, except your intelligence!" we exclaimed in unison.

He came to sit next to me as if I were a long lost friend. "I do not agree," he said, "with the Christian doctrine that man is born evil. I am of the idea of Jean-Jacques Rousseau that he is born good, but that society corrupts him." He smiled at me. "Furthermore, I love the tiny mole you have behind your right ear." He very slowly bent his head towards my ear and kissed me on the mole with tenderness and delicacy. His beard felt surprisingly soft.

The next morning I resigned from the FBI. I was definitely not cut out for the job.

Feline Enigma

Sylvie owns a cat, a Persian cat. She got it from the SPCA. It was born on a retired ship in Alameda, at an abandoned shipyard, and was a ball of matted fur, its long eyelashes stuck together, its paws bleeding. A volunteer, who was on duty for the "cat route," spotted the tiny creature, huddled behind the grand mast.

Sylvie brought the cat back to her Berkeley home, in the hills. Her live-in partner, Christophe, who was versed in French Letters, immediately baptized it Uzbek.

At first, Uzbek just stood, as if frozen, behind the elaborate cat climber, purchased before his arrival, but ventured out, from time to time, to sip a little milk with its adorable pink tongue. He had large blue-green eyes bordered with black kohl.

In the space of a few weeks, Uzbek had turned into a distinguished, slightly haughty gentleman with glorious white fur, daily and lovingly groomed, his nails clipped to perfection. Sylvie fed him a delicate mixture of duck liver and bacon bits and gave him rose petal water to drink in a bowl of exquisite blue ceramic. He had taken very quickly to Berkeley mores.

Due to a reminiscence of his birth in the wild, he insisted on going outside in the morning to survey his domain, the garden with its heirloom tomatoes, wild strawberries, and black tulips; and to catch sight of hummingbirds, which had become scarcer since his arrival.

One morning, Sylvie opened the kitchen door, where he was waiting to be let out. It was raining dogs in whole baskets, inundating the vegetable garden and Christophe's tulip patch. Uzbek retreated in horror, ran to the front door, which Sylvie opened. Deluge and flooding here too! Poor Uzbek! He turned his innocent and troubled flat face towards Sylvie as if she held the remedy. He jumped back; she slammed the door shut. Quietness and coziness took him back into her smooth, warm arms.

Since then, Uzbek stares out of windows.

Morgan & Co.

I never lent Morgan $400.

First, I don't know any Morgan, except J.P. Morgan. He is unlikely to want to borrow money from me. That would be the day!

Second, I don't have $400.

But, even if I had the money to spare and Morgan as a friend, I would have to consider if he were *truly* a friend. Has he ever lent me any money? Of course not! Not that I have asked; he never has anything.

One night, Morgan, seated at the bar of a gloomy saloon on Chestnut Street, would be nursing Johnny Walkers, one after the other, having just lost his rent money to poker!

"Look here, Morgan," I'd venture. "Why don't you get a job?"

He'd turn brusquely towards me, with an expression of infinite contempt in his inebriated, pale eyes. "Don't be so American!" he'd hiss, followed by an ingratiating, "Why don't you lend me $400, ducky?"

I would then expound my super-sad story to support my claim that I did not have $400. Of course, he would not be listening, so engrossed would he be in his financial problems.

But suppose he had been listening and said, "If you had $400, would you loan it to me?" The question would reveal an unexpected delicacy of feeling on his part. I would then be in a quandary, not wanting to upset him with my suspicion that he may not be a *true* friend.

We, the Passengers

Saturday afternoon, St Patrick's Day. The #45 bus is negotiating the chaos of Chinatown. Third stop on Stockton Street — old ladies with canes and tiny feet, middle-aged people with orange plastic bags, young people lost in their smart phones, laying siege to bus from front and back. Staccato-words, bits of information are exchanged amongst older immigrants. Cantonese, Vietnamese, Korean? Most of them have to stand, hanging by one hand.

Bus groans and moans. Oops, sparkle! Bus stops briskly and deflates with a pained sigh, a trolley pole has come unhooked from its wire. Sitting passengers jolted out of their seat, standing passengers receiving brunt of sitting passengers. Driver, wearing a green shirt, jumps out and rushes to back of bus. Adroitly puts spring-loaded pole back unto track. Sparkle, bus leaps up. Standing passengers swing lightly into each other. Driver back in saddle.

At last bus stop before Stockton-Sutter tunnel, a young blond tourist in shorts jumps up to exit and screams, "Back door, back door."

We, the passengers — Asians and Caucasians in unison — shout back, "Step down, step down."

Bus driver has stopped being cool, now hollers, "Lady, next time, ring the bell!"

Girl is frozen, although light over door has turned green. She doesn't understand why door doesn't open automatically.

"Step down." We scream louder. She does, unconvincingly as the door opens briskly to her surprise. Girl jumps out on sidewalk, with a dazed expression. We smile knowingly.

Bus driver reeling, jumping on his seat, shaking his head: "What times are these when passengers think I can read their minds? If I could, I wouldn't be driving a bus!" In great danger of rear ending a truck, he now turns around towards us, the passengers, "What do you all think?"

An eerie silence falls upon us, Asians and Caucasians alike.

The Time Fred Said He Was Going to the Car Wash

The other day — out of nowhere — my live-in partner said to me — his gaze avoiding mine: "Honey? I'm going to the car wash." I was *immediately* suspicious. You see, I was born in a country where men are known to say — out of nowhere: "Chérie, I'm going to get a pack of cigarettes." To wit, the unfortunate life partner thinks to herself: "Good riddance! No more stale ashes, no more burnt pillowcases, no more, no more."

Fred, being Californian, did not smoke cigarettes, only joints of fragrant marijuana grown organically on a lesbian commune in Humboldt County. He indulged so much while watching games on my flat screen TV that the whole household — myself and the dog included — were all agreeably stoned.

But when he made this pronouncement, I was stunned... because we didn't own a car. Being green, I favored public transportation, while Fred constantly grumbled about MUNI's mishaps or BART being on strike.

Was he implying that his dream had been fulfilled and that we were now *proud* possessors... of a car?

I decided to play along to see where it would lead us. "Oh, you mean the red Alfa Romeo I parked in the neighbor's place?"

It was his turn to look worried. "No, darling," he sneered. "You bought a Smart car because you said it looks cool and is easy to park. Plus, it's electric blue."

We were getting nowhere. But, now I was secretly wishing that Fred would *indeed* go for a car wash. And never come back. Car included.

Cleopatra's Nose

I am watering the geraniums on the windowsill of my apartment on the sixth floor. I am careful when I perform this task not to spill water down below, on the café's dog's nose, a black Sheppard named Cleopatra. When you go around her on the sidewalk where her lustrous body is sprawled, her large spongy nostrils quiver to sustain a constantly humid spot on the grey asphalt. A drop of cold water on that sensitive organ triggers agonized cries, which put the neighborhood on alert.

The water is quickly absorbed by the dry earth, which now re-settles with ease in the pots. All is quiet. I spy a ladybug on a pale green leaf. Its two bright orange elytra closed, now protecting the thin membranous wings, form a convex carapace shining between seven black dots.

Before splashing the leaf, I want to assure the ladybug's safety by transferring it to my neighbor's planter. I lean on my left leg, turn my torso to the left, while my extended right leg maintains balance; but the standing leg becomes entangled with the hose. Instinctively, I hop and go spiraling towards the sidewalk in Downward Facing Dog position. Silly isn't it?

The morning breeze, still unpolluted by traffic, feels soothing to the skin of my cheeks. As I descend, I begin to experience the world from a different perspective.

On the fifth floor, reception at the Albertins. A box of pink *dragées* interspersed with tiny golden beads is being passed around by hands without bodies. Elegantly dressed torsos lean over a frilly white crib, where a newly baptized child is in happy baby pose, show-ing off its bright pink gums to their wide adoring upside down smiles.

On the fourth floor, another reception: A girl dressed in a long white robe held at the waist by a simple cord; her auburn hair has been elaborately set up in ringlets. A woman is handing her a first

31

jewel: a medal embossed with the head of the Virgin on its chain, in delicate gold. Her father's old-fashioned camera is capturing the scene.

Third floor: glitter and happiness. The bride is wearing white. She is smiling at the groom, but he is looking sideways. He is wide-eyed, long-legged, bearded. Her mother is attending the ceremony; her father is absent.

Second floor: She is wearing a red dress — bright red lipstick. He has a knife in hand. She screams pitifully: "Murder! Murder!"

First floor: I cannot distinguish what is happening as my speed is increasing exponentially according to the law of terrestrial attraction. My eyes are closed in anticipation of the fatal moment where my skull will unceremoniously meet the pavement.

The shock is deadened by a spongy and wet substance. Cleopatra's nose! I bounce up, feet first this time, and rewind along the façade of the building. Time also reverses: Murder. Wedding reception. First communion. Baptism. I am back where and when I was, placing the coleopteran in the neighbor's planter. All is quiet.

Charade

It is about the size of a woman's hand and fits snugly into a jacket pocket. Slippery and cool, heavy, and dense. Its two main faces, parallel to each other, form rectangles. Two other faces, also parallel, are narrow and long. One of the larger faces forms in its center a perfectly round crater containing a ring, which encircles a square. At the bottom left of this surface the index finger reads YNOS, in mirror writing.

The two longest faces also present various inscriptions but indecipherable to the finger. However, one of these sides is outfitted with a round-angled parallelepiped, slightly elevated, responding easily to the touch. Now, the fingers feel a very small circle, as if chiseled out of the overall substance of which the object is made. The index finger deciphers the word P O W E R engraved next to the circle. The tip of the nail presses on the circle, presses again hard this time. The elevated apparatus — the crater cradling a ring encircling a square — swiftly jumps out into the hand.

A smooth rectangular surface take up most of the opposite face. Its texture is different than the other parts of the object, as glass is to metal. The fingers linger over a long oval shaped button with two slightly elevated sides. If you press on the right part of the button, the crater-like apparatus juts out with a sleek purr. If you press on the left side, it retracts.

You look around and spot a raven sitting on a branch of an oak, holding a round, soft looking cheese in its beak. A smooth looking fox is intently — almost amorously — gazing up at the raven. The object, whose cord is wrapped around your wrist, is warm and awake, ready to start hunting. Outside, it is chilly. You hesitate before taking it out of your pocket — you forgot your mittens. Too late. The raven crows and drops the cheese. The fox swiftly elopes with it. The object's cylindrical head goes back into its shell with a hungry hum.

The Bear Skin

A lazy finger came out from between two mauve satin sheets and pressed the alarm button of the clock. A few seconds later, a head endowed with a black and unruly crown of hair emerged: Steve Ludlow!

"Holy Shit! It's six am! Why did I turn on the alarm so early?" His forehead wrinkled in puzzlement. Steve had an appointment at nine am with an editor at Simon & Shuster, one of his father's former college roommates at Princeton. He had just finished a novel about a young American college boy during his junior year abroad in France. It was raunchy — à la Henry Miller, but also sensitive à la Anais Nin. The hero, Allen was discovering the power of women and sex. Both Allen and Steve were letting their hair down, as they would not have dared do in their native Boston.

Steve thought that every generation had its book. In the fifties, it was *Catcher in the Rye*, in the sixties *On the Road*, in the eighties, *American Psycho*. At the dawn of the 21st Century, it would be *How Tasty My Little American!*

His novel was a love story between a French prostitute, Artémise — who was also the narrator — and the protagonist, Allen. Steve had delighted getting out of his skin to lodge himself under a silky, fragrant one, taking on the voice of an urchin, cynical, savvy and lyrical. In the novel Artémise falls in love with Allen, although Steve's writing workshop fellows thought that turn most unrealistic.

The book would more than likely make the *New York Times* Bestseller List. Money, power, women. From then on, he would map out a stellar career, earning the Booker Prize, followed by the Nobel. The French government would make him *Chevalier des Arts et Lettres*. In his lifetime he would be published in the American Classics, become part of the Pantheon of American letters, and be buried with great pump in Montparnasse cemetery. Immortality would be awaiting him.

He felt a hot, excited tongue against his cheek, in long anxious licks: Fausta! He had to take her out before the inevitable happened. He sat up as if moved by a powerful spring, and glanced at the clock: it was ten am! He had missed his appointment! *Adieu,* glory!

When the Tree Came Down

I asked Sören if he would please pick the oranges from our tree, the trunk of which was bending dangerously towards the newly refurbished house of the town's lawyer. I had purchased, at the corner hardware, a long stick with a little wire basket at its end, called "orange picker" and handed it to him with a touch of melodrama. "Mañana," he said with a smile.

Was he being sarcastic? He had spent many years in Mexico as a migrant worker and told me that "mañana" was a code word for "never." When will you fix the roof? When will you mow the lawn? When will you mend the fender bender? Mañana, mañana, mañana.

That night was very windy. At 3:00 a.m, the attorney, a lanky fellow with a shaved head and striped pajamas, rang our doorbell. "Your frigging tree has created a crater in my house," he fumed. "I'll sue you for all you have."

The doctor who lived across the street came running out, scholarly looking and agitated. He had been sued by the lawyer for prescribing Viagra to him, after it failed. He was still sore from the experience and started to argue with the lawyer, saying that it was not the tree's fault, but his house's, which had not been remodeled according to code. He said the lawyer needed to sue the contractor, not us.

They were ready to come to blows. Sören, the dog and I were standing there, dumbfounded.

A few minutes later, the police — probably called by Miss Prescott, an insomniac spinster — were on the scene, flashing blue lights, redirecting traffic and rounding us all up.

Why, oh why, hadn't Sören done what I had asked him to do? Yesterday.

Woman in Prehistoric Landscape

The first time I saw a dinosaur, it was at the Museum of Natural History in New York on Central Park West and 79th Street. It took the form of a dirigible-like skeleton occupying the center of the Grand Hallway. It was half standing on its powerful hind legs, which had propelled it into long and high jumps over the meager vegetation in search of fresh flesh to dig its exposed and angry teeth into. Its head almost reached the high ceiling of the hallway; it rested on huge feet, creating tremendous echoes when it walked the surface of the earth. A very long spine extended into a tail at one end, and at the other into a long flexible neck, perfect for attack. It did not need to defend itself against any other creature. Is that why it became extinct, because it was too big for its britches? Or did it wait for that fateful comet to exterminate it?

I have heard that birds descend from dinosaurs. What were the evolutionary steps that led this monster into the exquisitely delicate hummingbirds I have seen in California? But of course, there are all kinds of birds, such as the vulture, with a head and neck devoid of feathers, the better to feast upon the innards of dead animals. Yes, I can see this bird coming from a dinosaur. It has the same purposeful look, as if it's entitled to be there, doing what it does without shame or remorse.

By the time the comet crashed into Earth, had some dinosaurs already been transformed into birds? One day, a dinosaur jumps off a cliff and — O, miracle! — stays up in the air, batting its front and hind legs. What did the dinosaur feel at that moment? Exhilaration at having conquered the skies or fear of soaring into the unknown with a weightless and disoriented body?

Are birds in the process of transforming again as climate change is menacing the planet?

And what shape will they take? And of course, the haunting and perennial question: What about man? How will his physical appearance change? Will he keep his mental ability, now that everyone is hooked to an electronic device? Will such a device be implanted at birth in the brains of infants, or even fetuses? Will technology save humanity from global warming? And what about all the other species? Will they disappear or adapt? Are they already in the process of adapting?

I read the label on the plaque of the immense skeleton: "Tyrannosaurus Rex." It said that the world of dinosaurs was a world without man, a world devoid of intent and illusion, a world of struggles and survival of the fittest.

I got out of there, slightly dazed, crossed the street and took a walk in Central Park.

Food for Thought

Last time I saw her was December 26th. As she was paying, she asked me if I had a good Christmas. I shook my head negatively. She was speechless for a short moment, but overcame her astonishment: "Oh! But your children did?"

I shook my head positively. "Oh yes, Madame Adrienne, my children did and my wife. Everybody had a good time, except me," I said putting on my saddest look.

She went, "Ooh! I am sorry to hear that!" Ah women! You can always count on them to be long on sympathy, but short on action… but why should I complain? After all she is quite charming.

The other day, I was holding my back with my left hand in the middle of an aisle of pasta, olive oil, anchovy paste. She passed me by, brisk as usual. "Your back bothering you, Angelo?"

I said, "Yes, I got up at four this morning to get the Fujis."

"And we all take it for granted!" she retorted. "We come in here without thinking how avocadoes and figs get here."

That made me smile. Now, here's an appreciative customer! Not like these school kids who invade the store at noon. They pick up packs of candies or cookies and throw them back in the wrong place. Sometimes, I even catch them, hands in the chocolate containers.

Yesterday, a kid, full of bravado, came in with two of his buddies. He didn't buy anything but as he was going out, I noticed he was walking slowly and stiffly as if he'd swallowed a broom stick. "Come here, boy!" I said sternly from behind the counter. He started shaking, a far cry from macho man who first came in. His friends, who were lingering in the back, were watching the scene with snide smiles, poking each other with their elbows.

As the trembling kid came towards me, ten identically sized cans fell out of the legs of his pants with a loud tinny sound. I said, "Why on earth are you stealing that?" If it'd been alcohol or cigarettes, I would have understood. But cat food?

The kid was sweating and stammered, "It's for Madame Adrienne."

"Madame Adrienne?" *My* Madame Adrienne? It was my turn to feel queasy. "Madame eats cat food?"

"Yes," continued the kid, "I'm her assistant. We feed feral cats in Oakland on her cat route."

"What!" I exclaimed. "Does she know you steal from Mayflower grocery?"

"Oh yes, she had the idea. She says that it's not a crime to steal for animals."

I was shaking my head in disbelief. Adrienne, that cute little lady!

"Yes," continued the boy. "She says animals need retribution from us humans because we have killed them and eaten them since the beginning of time."

"We've eaten cats?" I asked incredulously.

"She thinks that all animals, even pets, are linked to each other. You kill a cow; she steals a can of cat food."

Well, I'll be damned.

Moving is Moving is Moving is…

Eléonore's boyfriend moved in with her three years ago. Her place is bigger than the hotel room he inhabited on Place Dauphine with his ex. He had moved to Paris to be a writer like Hemingway, who roasted pigeons he captured in the Luxembourg gardens, and sautéed them in butter and garlic, on a gas burner, in his room under the roof.

She lived on rue Bréa, also under the roof, facing the Art Nouveau building on rue Vavin, with its recessed balconies and white ceramic façade neatly interspersed with blue tiles. From her little balcony you could see Sacré Coeur on a clear day.

The first year was enchanting. They ate oysters at *La Coupole* and were spotted dancing at *Chez Régine*. They went to smoky clubs and would emerge in the early morning as ghosts, stepping out into the pale grey Parisian air. He called her his Inspiration, his Respiration. She enjoyed being someone's Muse. The very thought that they might not have met made them shudder in unison.

But over the months, Siegfried had become sloppy and disgruntled. He spent hours staring in anguish at the murky screen of his computer, smoking a blend of hashish and tobacco, the smell of which made Eléonore nauseous. He insisted he was suffering from *agoragraphia*, a condition diagnosed by French Symbolists poets at the end of the 19th century, and even hinted that Eléonore had castrated him creatively.

Meanwhile, Eléonore, who was also a writer, was working at UNESCO, translating rambling speeches by African dictators from French into English, and from English into French.

One evening, she came home to find Siegfried drunk and stoned with a couple of the familiar bums who hung around their neighborhood. As soon as the trio saw her, joyful sounds came from their wobbly bodies, but these noises were not *really* for her as an irreplaceable human but because they were hungry and wanted her to cook pasta for them.

"Would you, darling?" asked Siegfried with an expression he thought would move her, but something she had grown tired of after he awkwardly tried to kiss her and stepped on Belle's paw. Belle, Eléonore's beloved Jack Russell, emitted an awful squeak, which stabbed Eléonore in the heart.

Eléonore had an epiphany. She knew it would be difficult to get Siegfried to move out, or rather, it would be impossible for *her* to ask him to hit the road and never come back. She never asked herself why because she would not have known the answer anyway. Why was Eléonore so afraid of asking Siegfried, who had been a prick for months, in her own apartment — and she had let it happen! — to hit the road, Jack?

The most elegant solution was for *her* to move out. She would thus be spared pitiful cries and murmurs of suicide. As a matter of fact, she had been thinking of changing neighborhoods for a couple of years now, even before she had the misfortune of having Siegfried lay his predatory eyes on her at Geneviève's party.

It was time to move on. She wanted a new beginning. At the same time, she resented that *she* had to move out. If only she had a little courage, she would just change the lock while he was out with his cronies and throw his things out the window, into the gutter.

She packed light; so did Belle. And while Siegfried, his frame spread-eagled all over the bed was snoring like a drunken peasant, Eléonore and Belle quietly left.

Eléonore walked deftly on the moist pavement. She was free now. The blue morning air caressed her cheek. Moving out: to flee, to fly, perchance to soar...

Moving in was trickier. Finding a place would not be easy. Were there any places left for Parisians to live, now that Paris had turned into a beautiful museum?

Neuroesthetics

It is night time. I am high on a tiny terrace enclosed by an iron balcony. Mommy is holding my arms up while I am testing the ground below with cautious but enthusiastic first steps. She has dressed me in that white and soft fur-like catsuit that I have seen myself wear in pictures. My cheeks are rosy and my eyes are grey. The air is fresh, a little smoky. Mommy is smiling. I am ready for the world.

Now we are at the railing of the balcony. Mommy lets go of my arms and wraps my hands around two iron rails. I grip; I take a deep breath and look down: A soft blanket of night hovers upon the city I will one day know as Paris. Undulating threads of silvery and golden lights twinkle in a slow and rhythmical ballet. I am suffused with a feeling of softness, kindness and enchantment.

I hold on tighter to the iron rail, and pointing an index towards the apparition, I whisper, "pretty, pretty," my first word! I turn my head towards Mommy. She is smiling her Mona Lisa smile.

Eléonore

There is something I meant to tell you," the young woman murmured after a while. Where had he seen this expression, assertive and uncertain at the same time? He stared at her. Could it be? Could she be?

She leaned towards him. "Do you remember that night in the park?" Sebastien was in shock. In his short life, he had experienced the most intense sexual encounter with Eléonore — his half sister, in the park of the manor where they were brought up. They had performed the dance of desire, and bathed by moonlight, had exchanged the most intimate and ecstatic caresses. Never to reunite again.

But what had happened to her? He thought she had died. How had she made her way to Honolulu from the ancestral manor in Brittany? But this was not Eléonore. Eléonore had porcelain skin, which she enhanced with a powder of mother-of-pearl. Eléonore had opaque black hair with hues of dark blue, like the plumage of the long extinct raven. This young woman's hair was lustrous with hints of burnt copper. Eléonore had large oval eyes; the young woman's were smaller, shaped like elongated triangles, and within them an intriguing little flame was burning.

At this moment, though, the expression in her eyes was the same he had noticed in Eléonore's when he passed her in the hallways, as if the owners of those eyes had experienced great harm and mischief in an ancient past. There's something I meant to tell you. Did he want to know? He was not sure. He wanted to stay in the playful and innocent present.

They found themselves lying on the beach facing the Pacific Ocean. There's something I've meant to tell you. He sealed her lips with a finger, and reopened them. Soon, she'll be floating over the sand, then the water, into the deep blue sky.

He woke up, on the beach. She had left. The shape of her body was still gently imprinted in the sand, soon to be eroded by wind and sun.

The Power of Printed Words

I was standing at the corner of Sutter and Powell, selling the Street Sheet, eight pm. People were ignoring me. Perhaps I was invisible; the fog was like thick cold soup. And darn it! A cop comes out of it, chewing gum, hand on his gun.

He says, "Ya got a permit?"

I says, "No, what for?"

He says, "For selling on the street."

I play dumb. "For selling on the street?"

The cop starts balancing on his heels. I can see he's on a short fuse. "I got to impound your papers."

"You got to do what?" I ask.

He's fuming now. He grabs the Street Sheets and tries to get them out of my hands. Most of them are out of date anyway, but it gives me some kind of cover. Tug of War for a while.

He pulls harder. The papers are damp and slippery; they're not tearing apart. Now he's dragging me up the tracks on Powell Street. I feel like my spine is being torn from my ribcage. I don't know what'll happen if one of those cable cars comes barreling down. He doesn't care.

I suddenly remembered what a Chinese fellow told me one night in a bar in the Mission: don't fight, let go.

That's what I did, and the cop fell on his ass. His head banged on the tracks. The tourists, who'd been staring at the scene, burst into laughter. I took a deep breath, rolled over to my side, stood up and beat it.

O Why Do I Love Paris?

The floor is made of shiny wood planks. The curtains have been drawn, hiding the somber winter light. She has put a 45 on the small phonograph. She sits on her bed, feet dangling; her dolls smile at her. Paul Anka is singing

I love Paris in the winter when it drizzles,

I love Paris in the summer when it sizzles,

I love Paris in the Spring time,

I love Paris in the Fall. They don't say the autumn in America; the Fall, what an interesting switch.

I love Paris every moment, every moment of the year. His voice takes on an irresistible tender intonation, *O why, O why do I love Paris?* How romantic! An American in Paris! Hemingway, Gertrude Stein, F. Scott Fitzgerald, Richard Wright, James Baldwin, Josephine Baker!

O why O why do I love Paris? He teases and croons. At long last he bursts out in a crescendo of triumphant music. *Because my love... because my love...because my love... because my love... is here!* How trite, how petty! How disappointing! She throws the record across the room.

But when she thinks about it, just asking the question, "Why do I love Paris?" is odd. Do you need a reason to love Paris?

Fooled You

When fools start tap dancing on the top of a pin cushion, their elevated heels sink into the soft pink. You can hear Gene Kelly tapping and Georges Guétary whistling to the tune of "S'wonderful" in the background. But for the fools, there is no pavement to bounce off and no tap tap… whatsoever.

The fools despair as the cushion disrepairs under the unctuous movements of their feet. They agitate their arms, like demented puppets, in an effort to unglue themselves from the fabric which transformed their once powerful heels into marshmallows.

The more they try to disentangle, the more they entangle themselves. To the extent that they run the risk of becoming prey to the material, as happens when the unfortunate traveler finds herself at dusk slowly digested by a swamp: eyes, ears, nostrils, mouth gulping.

A crystalline laughter accompanied by dainty footsteps on the parquet, preceded by a white fluffy ball adorned with violet eyes. Daphné and her Siamese cat, Eddie Puss. The girl, without thinking, picks up the pin cushion where our poor fools are still sinking. She throws it adroitly across the room for the kitten to catch and amuse himself.

The fools have gone from a rock (if one may analogically call the pin cushion a rock) and a hard place, literally and metaphorically.

Now on the parquet, they do have *a choice*: stay desperately glued to the cushion or make a prodigious leap to escape Eddie Puss' sharp claws and his cruel teeth.

Choice: the price of freedom.

The Laundrophone

For Bill

Adrian had worked all night on a project to create a "genius" phone with an app: "Wash Machine." This app would be designed with Techies in mind — at least in the beginning, but eventually for humans at large.

These Techies had emigrated from the Silicon Valley and now populated the South of Market area of San Francisco, although some were venturing into other parts of the city, such as North Beach and Pacific Heights, never leaving their cubicles, unaware of the weather, fit for the beach or breezy and cool. They never used public transportation, as they were transported to work in dark-tinted massive grey buses outfitted with treadmills and IPads. At lunch they fed themselves from vending machines — sliding their gold American Express for tofu sandwiches, herbal iced tea, espresso.

The Techies knew that if they didn't have to go to the Laundromat, they would have more time for technological creativity, allowing them to invent the App of all apps, which would do everything for us, perhaps even live our lives.

In order to use their modest-sized genius phones as washing machines, they would have to become much smaller than they were in order to accommodate smaller clothes. So now Adrian was thinking of a way to shrink humans. Why not? After all, humans were being cloned — illegally.

He recapitulated in his mind. Turning human-size creatures into genetically engineered midgets, which begat midget consumers and workers, would open virtual space for the creation of a phone with a washing machine app. These new humans would have to be outfitted with tiny designer jeans, T-shirts and Converses, which would give a giant boost to the economy. Furthermore, the shrinking of humanity would solve the problem of overcrowding, delaying perhaps the colonization of other planets by humans.

It dawned on him that if the human race were to be shrunk, the whole world with its inhabitants, animals, plants and pets also had to be reduced considerably in size. Otherwise, birds would appear to these downsized humans like dinosaurs and instill in them an ancestral fear. Humanity's creations, such as the Eiffel Tower, the Pyramids, and the Tower of Babel, would also have to go through a similar process. You wouldn't shrink Venice, however, due to its ecological fragility, but enshrine her as a Super Giant Disney Land.

Adrian turned off his IPad and wiggled comfortably into his sleeping bag, bringing it up to his chin, as dawn with pink fingers opened up the gates of day. He heard the loud clinking sounds of the garbage truck outside and got ready for eight hours full of wonders.

The Devil and Aunt Catherine

After the death of her husband, Léonard, Aunt Catherine took to her bedroom, afflicted with all kinds of ills. She resents commiseration, "yes, my poor lady it must be terrible never to go out," or the cheerful dismissal of others, "Oh, come on, let's go for a walk; it's a beautiful day." Papa says Aunt Catherine is neurasthenic.

I visit her on Sundays before mass. We drink Earl Grey tea with a touch of essence of bergamot. Aunt Catherine tells me how to make a good cup of tea and that the best tea is made in a metal pot.

She asks me what my favorite subject is in school. It's French, followed by English. I am terrible at Math (especially Geometry), Physics, Chemistry and Natural Sciences. I don't shine in Geography or History. She says it doesn't matter because I will get married one day to a person who will support my addiction to novels. My favorite is *Nausea* by Jean-Paul Sartre. My aunt shakes her head and asks me what I like about it with an air of not wanting to know.

One Sunday I arrive late, out of breath, as my aunt is a stickler for exactitude. When she opens the door, she always says: "Exactitude is the quality of queens." This time, she does not open her door. After a while, I take out my key and let myself in.

Aunt Catherine is standing at the window behind the white lace curtain, staring at the house across the street, the house of the parish priest, an unpretentious affair. She does not turn around to greet me; she says that she saw a woman dressed in pink silk enter the house of the priest two hours earlier. She says that she heard moans and sighs from the priest's house. I ask her if she called the police, which only consists of one man, M. Sauvadet, equipped with a handle-bar mustache and whispered to be a communist. Aunt Catherine smiles, a rare occurrence. She lightly blushes and says, "No, no dear. I don't think so, but God will punish him."

No sooner said, the sky, which was uniformly blue, turns dark grey. A flash of lightning illuminates the modest house in bright orange, thunder strikes clumsily. My aunt and I, who have retreated to the center of the room, go back to the window. It has stopped raining but it is difficult to distinguish anything among the rubble. We go out to the street, open the latch to the parish gate, and enter what is left of the domain.

There is no more outside or inside; crows are already hovering over the ruins. This had been the priest's kitchen, this, his tiny dining room. In what is left of the bedroom, we spot on the back of an armchair — which has miraculously survived the catastrophe — a corset of softly shining blue satin with matching lace garters, upon which lies a rosary of black beads, held together by an inverted cross. My aunt gasps. The sign of Satan! All this arranged with a sense of ineluctability, as in a surrealist composition.

My aunt and I walk out slowly. "Ah, she says," lifting pious eyes up to the imperturbable skies, "sometimes, God tests our Catholic beliefs." She smiles wanly. I kiss her on both cheeks and bid her *adieu*.

Louse

You crawl furtively onto an innocent girl-child's hair from that of her best friend, to whom she was confiding, and dig your claws into her delicate skin to suck her blood. You lay eggs and reproduce shamelessly on the head of the unfortunate child, who has been scratching her scalp furiously these last few days, even as she is being admonished by her father to stop immediately or else. Louse, son of dirt, you thrive in dark and quiet places to spread contagious diseases such as exanthematic typhus.

Scientists say that when a hungry louse sticks its proboscis into a blood-vessel, blood gushes into its intestinal tube with such rapidity and abundance that the observer recoils from his microscope.

The early walker, as he crosses the countryside, will often notice a young child with thick red hair sitting on the windowsill of a cottage. Two older girls, his sisters probably, are gently bending his neck and with long white fingers, dancing over his head, hunting for lice. The air outside is silvery blue.

The boy is not quite awake, half of his body still in the warm dark bedroom and the other bathing in the chill of early morning. He hears the song of his sisters' breath interrupted by slight whistles as they catch their saliva. He hears their fragrant lashes flutter and the crackle of tiny insects crushed to death between vengeful and silvery nails.

O louse, 19th century French icon!

At school all scalps have been scrubbed with vinegar. A faint and pungent odor lingers in the ranks as we assemble to start the day.

The hair of the little girl in front of me is usually unremarkable, but today it has reflections of bronze, orange and yellow. She has the hair of Helen of Troy, for whom men spilled blood.

I have very fine long hair; in the mornings it is matted. After our bath, lovingly administered by Mommy, my squeaky clean hair cascades over a plaited robe. I am smiling at Papa's camera, although I have suffered for this result. The boar's hair brush, squarely placed in the right hand of a no-nonsense country woman, has tortured me for an hour. My hair is full of tiny knots, and the implacable instrument has made my eyes red and teary. "Please stop!" I scream. The torture will end only when all the knots have been detangled. At the end of the torment, my cranium is prickling. It's bleeding; icy, yet on fire. My nerves are raw and retracting.

I do not remember furiously scratching my scalp. Not that I would be ashamed of it. Having lice was not disgraceful and almost a badge of honor. It must have something to do with the French paradox.

Marvin in the Morning

Surprisingly, I woke up this morning. My head felt cold, a result of premature balding. I was feeling lonely. You'd think that by now, being a shrink, I would have resolved my psychological problems. How can you cure people when you yourself are a loony? Or maybe you have to be afflicted with the same shortcomings as your patients in order to understand them better?

Yes, I was lonely and I was paunchy. So, get married, you'd say! No, I'm committed to be single forever. I promised my mother on her death bed. She looked at me imploringly with her big brown eyes. "Marvin," she said, "never get married. Promise!" How could I deny a dying mother?

She loved me and I had an Oedipal longing for her. Last night, I dreamed that we were getting married. She wore a white dress with orange blossoms in her raven hair. She was young and beautiful. Unfortunately, the dream turned into a nightmare because as soon as the ceremony was over, she became Mother again.

I have had some girlfriends, even a steamy French one. Her name was Eléonore. We would picnic naked in Central Park and play Venus and Mars during our siestas. But one day, she looked straight at me with her expressive dark eyes, as we were having breakfast at the kitchen table and she said to me, "Marvin, I like you very much, but I can't be your lover *and* your mother at the same time!" She kissed me on both cheeks and just left, never to be seen again.

So I took to writing psychoanalytical books, to counteract Deleuze and Guattari's *Anti-Oedipus: Capitalism and Schizophrenia.* So French!

But to get back to our story, I didn't sleep much after this dream but did manage to get out of bed. I made myself some coffee and perused the *New York Times'* bestseller list. If only I could see my name and the title of my new book there, *Is Oedipus Online?* I would be happy!

Unwritten Note
for Jodi Hottel & Roger Shimomura

I am riding the tricycle Papa made for me out of old wheels he found in the dump. I roam among sharp black and blue barracks. Brown clouds hover over the camp, and in the distance, I can see the mauve hills around Mount Minidoka. I am lonely yet not alone.

I do not want to turn around to see what Papa calls the American Guardian. I know he is watching me through binoculars. He wears a helmet, and a shotgun hangs on his shoulder. Would he shoot if I made a dash towards the barbed wires, towards freedom?

I feel very small and he is large and black, like an Angel of Death, says Mama. He is the American Enemy. Will I have an American Guardian over my shoulder watching me all my life?

But am I not an American? Could I become an American Guardian myself?

Would I watch over my parents to make sure they didn't escape?

About the Author

Michèle Praeger's three previous lives read like a French childhood memoir, an absurdist comedy, and a Henry James novel. In her present life, she lives and writes in San Francisco.

www.ingramcontent.com/pod-product-compliance
Lightning Source LLC
Chambersburg PA
CBHW032035090426
42741CB00006B/826